With this debut collection, Jesse Butler is joining the growing group of Canadian poets who are taking poetry away from the academy and returning it to a broader audience of poetry lovers. Butler's poems are thoughtful, well-crafted, and a pleasure to read.

A. M. Juster, author of *Wonder & Wrath*

+++

This is a very fine book. Jesse Butler has put his mastery of traditional poetic form to good use in these varied reflections on faith, personal tragedy, encounters with nature, life in the modern Canadian suburbs and many other things. These poems reveal a mind expansively curious about the world and deeply attentive to it.

Burl Horniachek, editor of *To Heaven's Rim: The Kingdom Poets Book of World Christian Poetry*

+++

It's not so often that a debut collection of poetry reveals a care for poetic forms, a clarity in book structure, and a serious grappling with large ideas. Jesse Keith Butler's ambitious **The Living Law** reaches for the large: a world that lacks its Blake to etch fire in the mind; makeshift shelters in a modern landscape stripped of spirit and transcendence; the pulse of life below the world's veneer; the living law as gateway onto a wide, windswept expanse. (And don't miss the hermit's donkeys!)

Marly Youmans, author of *Seren of the Wildwood*

The Living Law

Poems by

Jesse Keith Butler

darkly bright press

The Living Law
Poems by Jesse Keith Butler

Catalog Number 019

ISBN: 979-8-9899449-0-3

Library of Congress Control Number: 2024930881

Publisher's Cataloging-in-Publication data

Names: Butler, Jesse Keith, author.
Title: The living law / poems by Jesse Keith Butler.
Description: Cochiti Lake, NM: Darkly Bright Press, 2024.
Identifiers: LCCN: 2024930881 | ISBN: 979-8-9899449-0-3
Subjects: LCSH Canadian poetry--21st century. | BISAC POETRY / Canadian |
POETRY / Sonnets | POETRY / Subjects and Themes / Inspirational & Religious
Classification: LCC PR9199.4 .B88 2024 | DDC 811.6--dc23

darkly bright
press & design

www.darklybrightpress.com

Table of Contents

Dedicated to the recently departed:

Chris Butler,

Carl Squires,

Clarence & Muriel McDonald.

May their memory be eternal.

Immanence

                                        the eyes
of the watcher altered and faltered and again saw
the primal Nature revealed as a law to the creature

                                        —Charles Williams

The Living Law

Our bus leaves the prairies. I'm done with the flatness
that stretches for days without break.
Those long strained horizons are too much to witness.
Your eyes and your mind start to ache.

The landscape breaks out into ridges and gullies,
with purpose shown through every flaw.
Some days you can scrape back the world's shallow polish,
and glimpse at the wisdom at work in its fullness:
                            a deep and
                                        living
                                                law.

My self-respect slowly begins to unravel.
I've worn these same clothes now for days.
The sun's dropping down till it's right at eye-level.
I try, but I can't meet its gaze.

It's as round and austere, and with edges as sharp,
as the blade of a circular saw.
But I watch its geometry soften and warp
as it meets the horizon to gently absorb
                            beneath the
                                        living
                                                law.

The passengers all hold this suffering in common.
They're bound by the comforts they lack.
A soft even darkness has fallen, but someone
keeps snoring a couple rows back.

Well, sometimes I'm eager for human encounter,
but most of the time I withdraw.
On days like today I'm a lonely dissenter—
it's like I don't know that we're all living under
                            the one same
                                        living
                                                law.

An old woman's searching the floor with a case.
She asks for help finding her teeth.
I want to turn back from her big earnest face,
but I'm held by the life underneath.

We wake here and struggle to shape a response,
all tangled in hunger and awe.
But then something cuts through the dull resonance
and draws us to join a reciprocal dance
                    and love the
                             living
                                     law.

Beneath the Buzzing of My Brainstem

Beneath the buzzing of my brainstem breathes
an unseen life—an inner light-source, pure
and pulsing as the seared shell of a star—
unblurred, blossoming, bellowing heat. Beneath

my surface stirring swells a silent ocean—
as subtle as the tide singing through a seashell—
unsounded, unfathomed breadth shoring this brittle
crust of consciousness from crumbling, from crushing

its own mass to sand. There's so much I never see,
while I scamper after some new stimulus—
short-circuiting through the swirling shallows. Unless
my grip is loosened. Unless you lessen me—

and, for a moment of expansive quiet,
I feel the fist that holds my heart in its hollow
unclench, and unspanned space comes spilling through—
as my ribcage opens, like a flower to the light.

The Boatwright

For Chris Butler (1973-2022)

My brother, when I saw you lie
so still, I thought you must be gone.
The man I knew seemed distant on
the day we watched you die.

When you were here with us, your deft
hands couldn't stop creating. Will
we ever find a way to fill
this stillness that you've left?

Will you find something new to make?
You've been a carpenter, a chef,
an artist with a sailboat if
you met wind on the lake.

All movement stopped except your pulse,
and then your pulse went silent too.
I couldn't help but picture you
in movement someplace else.

You've never had much patience for
a problem that you couldn't get
your hands on. There are needs unmet
on earth. Why look for more?

But if you thought that we were quaint
for how we talked about our faith,
it didn't show. You took it with
the patience of a saint.

Indulge me one last time. I may
know less than you do now. But if
there's open water past this life
I know you'll find your way.

I see your smile, your sure resolve
in facing what's beyond the shore—
a new uncharted challenge for
your skillful hands to solve.

In all that ocean, you will be
in busy silent peace—afloat
and certain-footed in the boat
you're building on the sea.

Highway 17 Revisited

& behind him the hundred Inevitables made of solid rock & stone

—*Bob Dylan*

I thumbed a ride down where the eastbound lane
droned, glinting, gaunt, to greet the granite dawn—
an old man, driven back to days now gone
of *making love or else expecting rain.*
Bob Dylan moaned *a melody so plain*
on stereo, as we left Nipigon.
We'd hauled our memories to that place. Dragged on
behind, they cried out like the morning train.

The past would take its necessary course
on Highway 17, revisited.
Old choices petrified to reinforce
the bedrock. Dead rock surged up at its source,
and pulsed and pulled the rippling road. We sped
straight for that blunt horizon of remorse.

The Ladder

"Look," he says, "the friggin' Rocky Mountains." He lifts a hand from the wheel to gesture, and for a moment I could swear I see a twinkle of starlight through it, from the darkness out past the windshield. But now all that light is moving, concentrating itself on one of the icy mountaintops, and if he is still talking I no longer hear him. My gaze is held ahead and to the right, where the starlight crowning the mountaintop gathers itself up toward the cold heavy sky, into a column or maybe even a stairway, but moving, rolling upward like an escalator. And what's moving are actually particular shapes, monstrously huge, at times looking almost human in form, but strangely proportioned, at times looking more like shaggy shifting beasts. But they are all made of light and move like a river and the distinctions between them seem to blur in and out. And there is music too, or something like music, I can barely make it out but it makes my ears ache and convulses my gut into a sob of strange joy. My eyes stream with tears and I want to plug my ears and close it out and I wish I had a voice big and inhuman enough to sing along. I'm certain it's beautiful, but with a beauty that's pitched just too high for the human ear. It's the creatures on the ladder that are singing, I know that now, and they're both ascending and descending on a ladder whose end vanishes between the stars. I'm no longer aware of the car, or even of the mountains. The light, the song, is drawing me in. Somewhere, far away, I can feel my forehead pressed against the cold glass of the passenger-side window, the seatbelt digging into my neck. But if this is a dream, I'm not sure that I've ever been awake.

Sunrise Over Crow Puddle

When dawn reaches rosy fingers
between the criss-crossed tree branches
along the street that meets our house,
she swirls her colours through the water
that's puddled in our sagged cul-de-sac
like an artist washing paintbrushes.
Here a local crow comes back each day
bringing his breakfast of garbage to eat:
perhaps discarded sandwiches
or a desiccated mouse.

And watching, I almost forget to finish
my coffee. Somehow, I'm always surprised
to discover the subtle range of richness
an unremarkable moment can hold.
In all the houses down our block
the neighbours bustle about their business
as this crow gulps down his carrion
from a chalice of rose-gold.

Mid-Lent

we swing from June to June
— Terrance Hayes

The springtime here is overrated. Christ
was right to choose a warmer climate. Is
it really likely that he would have risen
so quickly, if he'd first descended from
a place like this? The backed-up sewers, the
decaying snowdrifts—everything smells dead.

Each spring my driveway floods. I'm down there, trampling
the solid ice the snowplows have packed down
along the curb, to find the drain. The death
of fall is heavy in the air, cut by
the thawing dog turds—one more scent of death.

I'm hacking at the ice. The stagnant and
disturbing water glups and slops upon
my clothes. At last: a crack and gurgle. Those
uncertain eddies slowly circle in
the water at my feet. I look up. The
receding snow holds little hollows—tombs
of winter muck. But underneath, bestowing
such unexpected hope, there is new life.

The Eleventh Hour

On Great and Holy Saturday night,
I'm at the children's hospital,
cradling your long, limp weight—
you've rarely seemed so little.

We're here amid the side effects
of a world that's suddenly sickened:
the clouded eyes above the masks,
the reek of disinfectant,

the makeshift surge wards. And down below
it all, a soft and holy hum—
the resurrection that's singing up through
the cold linoleum.

A Strand of Sound

I passed out and face-planted on my fourth full day of COVID.
You know this. I was feeling woozy, staggering for the couch,
then all was blackness. But before the trickle of sensation—
the painful pressure of the floor, the panicked footsteps rushing,
the focusing confusion, and the blood-taste in my mouth—
I found my name, a strand of sound, in your voice, my beloved.

I'd never known the secret strength that's hidden in a name
till passed-out and face-downward on my fourth full day of
    COVID—
like how the name of Lazarus was called into his tomb.
Before I slowly stirred and rose up in our living room,
I found my name—stray strands of sound—in your voice, my
    beloved.
The voice was just as vital. Only you could call me home.

The only line of clarity was climbing back to you
through depthless, deathless stillness spreading without shape or
    scope
while passed-out and face-downward on my fourth long day of
    COVID.
I found my name. Its strands of sound filled your voice, my
    beloved.
They gathered up through darkness like a tender, tangled rope
when life was lost in silence and this love was all I knew.

The Plague of Frogs

Tonight the plague of frogs comes in its turn.
And, just to earn their silence, as I pass,
I raise up ghosts of memory from the grass,
and offer up another town to burn.

This landscape has been judged. I'll find its fault.
The cities of my past will rise in flames.
My weakness is I'll still recall their names,
and scar my tongue with bitter pangs of salt.

The plague has come. But what the plague reveals
is what will haunt me when the plague is done.
Tonight I only hope I can outrun
the fire and brimstone blistering my heels.

The Red Sun Rising

Come down into the street to see the sunset on the city.
This world's unwell—a withered shell—but damn sometimes it's
    pretty.
The light spreads through the city smog, through thick and toxic
    air,
then manifold, in red and gold, it shimmers through your hair.
We've had our age, my love. We've had our centuries of leisure.
But in the earth they swelled to birth with deadly building pressure.
We've burned through all our stockpiled days. Their smoke fills the
    horizon.
Come. Night descends and, when it ends, we'll watch the red sun
    rising.

Come down into the street to see night settle on the city.
This metropolis's populace is drained and strained of pity.
Come, bring your lamp, your fiery sword, examine every face.
But honesty has gone to seed, and truth has left no trace.
If you find twenty righteous, will that stem the flood of sulphur?
If your sifting finds just fifteen will the flames remain uncalled-for?
But no one stands to meet your gaze. We scamper from the crisis.
We're thick with wealth and sick with self. And soon the red sun
    rises.

Come down into the street to see dawn strangle through the city,
through tangled bends and angles mapped out by some lost
    committee.
The light chokes through dark alleyways, but then bursts clean
    above
dim avenues we haven't used since we were first in love.
Come. Hold me close. Each surface this light touches it reclaims.
The earth still writhes with other lives. We've never learned their
    names.
We know what our life is, but not the weight of all it isn't.
So brace your sight to face the light, and now the red sun risen.

Lightning Strikes Churches

After Søren Kierkegaard

A church is a makeshifted shelter, a lean-to
thrown up against heaven, a wobbly but warm
enclosure that all the unready rush into
before the sharp edge of the storm.
When lightning strikes churches,
the pigeons know why.
They burst from their perches
and soar in the churchyard's blank sky.

A church is a fistful of feelings—its steeple
a finger unflinchingly jabbing at clouds—
enclosing the longing the righteous can keep all
their rightness, unreached by the crowds.
When lightning strikes churches
it feels out our worth,
then, finding no purchase,
it dissipates into the earth.

A church is a monument, far out of fashion,
that clings to the crumbling brink of the land,
a ritual built between Isaac's cold question
and Abraham's trembling hand.
When lightning strikes churches
it surges with light
and restlessly searches
for faith formed unbent in the night.

A church is a boat with a broad bow to carry
the last lines of life through the world-wasting flood,
a gunnel-thin wall between us and the fury
that's frothing and foaming our blood.
When lightning strikes churches
it shudders our core.
The ship leaps and lurches
then leans to the unsighted shore.

The Root of Jesse

This is he who was in the congregation in the wilderness with the angel who spoke to him at Mount Sinai, and with our fathers; and he received living oracles to give to us.

—Protomartyr Stephen

The Lawgiver

א

Blessed are the blameless who live in your law
The strong single-minded   The simple who focus
Toward this one purpose they half understand
While my skin was seared with the glory I saw

Blessed are those who walk steady and clear
The highway you've sliced through the wide wilderness
Blessed are those   If they've ever existed
I've kept your commands   Don't abandon me here

ב

The young will be true when they serve you alone
And give up their government to no other gods
With seventy elders I crested your mountain
You stood on a pavement of sapphire stone

We looked upon God   We ate and we drank
Then you called me into your flickering cloud
I stayed forty days as your fire filled my mind
Don't let the markings you've made there grow blank

ג

O Lord let me live and I'll follow your word
Uncover my eyes to the splendour of your law
Your presence expanded and spiralled above me
All alone on the mountain   My strained vision blurred

I cowered in the cleft   In the grasp of your grace
While the shadow of your glory singed the grass off the slope
I would rather be ashes than fade from your presence
I'm a stranger on earth   Please don't hide your face

ד

Raise me up with your word from the grip of my grave
My despair has brought me down to the dust
Give me life in your law   Lift this dead leaden weight
The gods we've imagined won't manage to save

I ground up their sin and I forced them to swallow
They gagged and gasped as they guzzled it down
I watched you withdrawing deep into the desert
But leave us the wake of your wisdom to follow

ה

Turn our eyes away from empty desire
And let us live again in your way
We've known your reproach   The earth opened wide
The unearthly snakes slithered up spitting fire

On the way from Mount Hor to the Red Sea
I cast your bronze serpent and lifted it up
Set your servant firmly in your word
In your goodness give life again to me

ו

Stretch your love out to me steadily strung
With precision   Like fire in an unburning bush
You don't speak in vain   I am who I am
Don't take your word of truth from my tongue

My uncovered feet found wide open space
West of the wilderness   On the mountain of God
Now I'll testify to your name before kings
And hold up unhidden my unburning face

ז

This is my comfort when the world goes dim
That you will remember your promise to me
That your angel will lead me where I have not gone
That he won't turn back   That your name's in him

The wicked and lawless fill me with spite
I'll hold no other god's name in my voice
In the night of pilgrimage I'll tell of your law
I'll remember your name in the outrushing light

ח

Lord you're the portion that we'll preserve
We'll gather our ration of bread at sunrise
Enough for the day and to keep your sabbath
We'll walk in your way   Now we won't swerve

What was it we hoarded a portion of
Writhing with worms now like rotted flesh
But dawn brings new mercy fine as hoarfrost
The earth brimming full with your fathomless love

ט

Your grace has brought me to the sabbath of your year
Ground me in sound judgment and the knowledge of your law
We hurriedly ate our chewy cuds of bread
The destroyer turned back at the doorway's blood-smear

Without your correction I'd be wandering still
With the wicked in the land whose hearts clog with fat
They screamed out at midnight clutching cold sons
It's good that I've suffered to bring me to your will

You built me from a breath and abandoned me in water
Shipwrecked and shivering in a bitumen basket
The righteous will see me raised up and rejoice
At the rise of the son of the sungod's granddaughter

The godless oppressors will wither and withdraw
When your pure judgment upends their strength
Build me tall as a beacon for the lost to look to
And trellis my will to the height of your law

כ

My soul is stretched on a framework of bone
My eyes shrivel watching the sunken skyline
For the distant speck of the storm of your wisdom
Your law is too heavy for me alone

The priest of Midian watched me withstand
The shrieking lawsuits   The failure of judgment
Father in law teach me how to be humble
In your love lengthen my life in your land

ל

You've anchored the earth to heaven's roofbeam
You've fixed it to freeze flow flood at your word
You stiffened the water like cliffs on each side
You stiffened their hearts as they rode down that seam

I didn't know what my hand trembled for
Out over the sea that reddened with daybreak
And waterlogged corpses   I shuddered but looked
At the breadth of your law   It had no far shore

מ

I've loved your law   I've turned each command
To see every side   To saturate my mind
To fill me with wisdom above my enemies
Crushed underfoot and hidden in the sand

Our secrets will be seen in blazing day
When they ask who stood me here as judge
I stand on sand that's as certain as stone
Your commandments steer me from every false way

נ

Your law rings its light on my stumbling path
I've sworn an oath and I will obey
You came to kill me when I stopped to rest
I shriveled before your unexplained wrath

She smears me with our son's skin and begs
That you bend your mercy on her bloodied bridegroom
She holds my quivering life in her hands
Now I'm braced to obey to the bitter dregs

ס

Evil swarms a man's mind like a hive
I've shielded my Cushite wife from their words
Now hold me high the way you promised
The humblest man who's here alive

You never let those who stray draw near
We threw my sister from the camp like filth
She questioned my calling   And called down your judgment
And her trembling flesh decayed in fear

ע

Extract us from under oppression intact
We've waited here doing what we thought was right
They heap up new burdens too heavy to bear
Your blessing's been blemished   Now it's time to act

You wore down their will so they wouldn't withhold
Their wealth from their slaves   We'll rob them ragged
Their bronze and silver   Their blue and scarlet
We'll hold your law precious   Much more than pure gold

פ

The lines of your teachings stretch taut and true there
The mountain alight with your unfolding words
But now I must harness this stiffnecked people
To build the designs you've drawn through the air

You stirred up their hearts   Each morning they came
With fine twined linens   With tanned rams' skins
My sight smears with tears when I see this abundance
These people returning   What's yours you will claim

צ

Your enemies never remember your word
It eats me alive   In anger I asked
To go three days' journey into the desert
To make you an offering there on the third

They wouldn't believe that we went to serve you
In a far fallow land that your faithfulness fills
With our wives and children   With our wealth and cattle
To test out your promise   To prove your law true

ק

I called from my core as the darkness increased
I crept past each boundary marked in the sand
Trying to touch the future you'd taught us
A state where each citizen stands as a priest

You're near to us   All your commandments are true
Past the base of this mountain you've built up forever
Where our promises hung   With withering heat
When we told you whatever you'd spoken we'd do

ר

Deliver me Lord for your mercy is just
This campful of cravings is too much to carry
I watched them eat meat till it oozed out their nostrils
I looked on their faithlessness then with disgust

You spread out your spirit through seventy hearts
Dispersing my burden   They burst out in blessings
And echoed your word that's endured forever
The sum of your mercy in each of its parts

שׁ

The land opened outward   A graspable gift
I welcomed your word like the wealth of conquest
We bravely brought back the fruit that we found
Its weight was almost too much to lift

But they crushed us like insects   We had to escape
The good broad land that you'd promised to us
And the peace of those who love your law
We wanted your blessing   But bent to our shape

37

ת

From the peak of Pisgah I've glimpsed paradise
Just let me live and I'll sing out your praise
You've only begun to show me your glory
Reach your hand out to lift me   I'll let this suffice

It was always a mountain   Each time that I saw
Your mercy unmasked in its broad barren beauty
When you found me   A lost sheep searching for shelter
On the long leeward slope of your steep windswept law

Villanelle of the Elect

So Jacob was loved, and Esau was hated.
It seems like a bit of an uneven deal.
You won't stop creating this world you've created.

If Esau had hope it was quickly deflated.
The subtle supplanter had him by the heel.
But Jacob was loved, and Esau was hated.

Outside of the city, with heaven ungated
and rungs reaching down, Jacob glimpsed what was real—
you still were creating this world you'd created.

Poor Esau found Jacob's thin soup overrated
when robbed of his birthright for one meatless meal.
Yet Jacob was loved, and Esau was hated.

You grappled with Jacob. He grunted and grated
while you danced, delighted to meet with such zeal
as you kept creating this world you'd created.

There's purpose in life but the path isn't fated.
You unspool these urgings we don't even feel.
And Jacob was loved. And Esau was hated.
You keep on creating this world you've created.

After Psalm 73

You brushed us off in anger, God.
          Why are you still unbending?
When can we hope to find an ending
          to our cold disgrace?
These scheming men rose in your place
          who damn themselves with doubt.
They desecrate your temple, Lord—
          When will you stomp them out?

They smile as they blast down the walls
          that once braced up our hymns.
We hide till the explosion dims—
          so terrified and frail.
We beg you for a sign, but fail
          to see the greater danger—
that any prophet sent now might
          walk past us like a stranger.

You've been our God so long now
          the beginning isn't clear.
You've always worked salvation here,
          right in the tumbling world.
You stemmed the surging sea, and hurled
          the creatures of the deep
back from the borders of the land
          to their forgotten sleep.

You stretched the seasons out through time
          to leave us space to live.
You open up each day and give
          the gentle closing night.
But cruel houses hoard their light
          and drench the dark with shame.
Please lift us like before, and let
          the fallen thank your name.

Hospitality

1.
This valley, where you called me, and I came,
is cold tonight. A sharp wind whips my clothes
and stings my eyes. I squint through burning tears
to see the land, the pulsing hills of grass,
you promised to me long ago. I wait
here in a place I live but cannot claim.
When you first called me from my father's house,
I overturned my life to follow you.
I was still young and hungry for your presence.
I'm old now, but the hunger is the same.

You gave me little glimpses of your glory,
but years apart. On your last visit here,
a man but so much more, you filled my doorway.
You bowed your head to enter, but the frame
still strained to take you in. I feared the food
I served would turn to ashes on your tongue.
You ate it anyway. I grew confused:
was it one man or three that sat before me?
I wasn't sure who hosted whom—your mercy
expanding to embrace my shallow shame.

Our generations rise and fall before you
like surging waves run through the fields of grass
and ripple down the landscape of your promise
beneath this violent wind. Our conversation
has just begun. My lifetime was a greeting.
I'll wait out my slow days here for your answer,
here in a place I live but cannot claim—
this valley, where you called me, and I came—
and hope for when my children's children's children,
some distant day, will get to hear your name.

2.

At each new time you turn away and leave
us here beneath the fallout of your promise,
there's something new that's lost. Now it's my sight
that fades before me day by day. My sons
are lost in their resentments, while their birthright
decays unclaimed. I sit here in the dark,
alone, my life now used up waiting for
a word that never came. My trembling hands
are empty. Somehow still it always seems
there's some new loss to gather up and grieve.

My father's gone now too. I've always felt
that something cracked inside him on that mountain,
while I lay there upon his makeshift altar,
hogtied and terrified. He spoke to you—
I only heard half of the conversation—
and somehow seemed to earn us a reprieve.
I memorized him, lying in his shadow:
His knuckles white around the knife. His eyes
so full of faith and terror and resolve.
The secret tears he smeared into his sleeve.

I have been faithful. Anything you said
to do I did. You never did say much.
And each new time you turn away and leave,
I sit here, with the darkness weighing in,
and sift among the shards left of your promise
for some new loss to gather up and grieve.
My birthright spent. My fractured father. My
embittered sons, both chosen and unchosen.
And this undying struggle—to believe
your grace is bigger than what we receive.

3.
Somewhere beneath the name I gave this place
lies what I saw here. Two encampments, both
alive with preparation in the shadow
that stretches from the mountain of our oath,
both nested in the slow bend of the river.
Two encampments, mine and yours, but somehow
they seemed to fill out one expanded space.
Two worlds that flickered in and out of focus,
diverging and converging in an instant,
so intricate in how they interlace.

You haunt me. You are everywhere I look,
yet nowhere. Now I've learned to always test
reality, to see if it holds firm.
That day I came to steal your blessing, bringing
that rich red stew, my cleverness fell from me
like skin. I stood there, with my lie laid bare.
Just then I saw my purpose joined to yours—
they seemed to meet in one expanded space.
You blessed me, like you always do, then left me
alone again to grapple with your grace.

I found you here tonight, well after darkness,
and hauled you to the ground. You wrenched my leg
to dislocate my hip. I howled with pain,
but held you here unmoved until you blessed me.
You never said your name. It's still there, hidden
somewhere beneath the name I gave this place.
It doesn't matter now. Dawn gleams across
the river. I rise, limping now, but ready
to find you in the daylight and embrace
the God that greets me from my brother's face.

Praise Him with Clashing Symbols

Praise the Lord up where the sky rests
its weight through the land and the sea.
Sun and moon, stars in the highest—
he spoke and this all came to be.

Praise the Lord, fruit trees and cedars,
reptiles that writhe in the deep.
Stormy winds—bend where he orders
the bounds you're created to keep.

Praise the Lord, croaking and trilling,
creeping things, high flying birds.
Young women, old men, and children,
lift out your splintering words.

Our thin rationality crumbles
whenever it reaches to him.
Yet praise him with clashing symbols
that dance out on language's rim.

Songs of Unrest

I say more: the just man justices

—Gerard Manley Hopkins

A Hermit's Elegy

We heard there was a hermit. What we heard
was mixed and muddied, muttered in the hall.
The monks were kind enough, but secrets stirred
in empty rooms. It made me think a person
might want a life of silence after all.

We heard there was a hermit. Once we had,
our boredom drove us out to go and see.
The monastery guesthouse wasn't bad.
But we were young. We hadn't quite stopped searching
for something bigger that our lives could be.

Our path to find the hermit thinly wound
through forests and around a golden field.
Then, just before a clump of hills, we found
a house of corrugated plastic sheeting.
We went to see what wisdom it concealed.

The man we found was stooped and frail. His beard
was grey and, in his army surplus hat,
he looked a bit like Castro. What was weird
to me though was the joy with which he welcomed
us in, and gave us mismatched chairs. We sat.

We started asking questions then. We hoped
for rich and ringing words that would restore
our grounding in the world, for words that scoped
the secrets of the soul. But he said little.
His eyes and voice trailed off toward the door.

He gave us each a chipped enamel cup
of water, while our words hung in the air.
When we ran out of questions, he lit up.
He asked us: "Would you like to meet my donkeys?"
I swear that old man jumped out of his chair.

He ran outside and called them each by name:
"Hosanna! Hallelujah!" Through a cleft
between two hills the bounding donkeys came.
He told us all about the care of donkeys.
We listened for a while and then we left.

We left in disappointment. Our complaint
was vague though. He was kind to us, but we
just weren't convinced that we had met a saint.
We stumbled through that landscape like two tourists,
discounting anything we couldn't see.

What was he doing, while he lived so long
in solitude? Just watching donkeys graze?
Perhaps that's it. But maybe I was wrong
to think that holiness is heard in thunder.
Perhaps it shows in unexpected ways.

Perhaps he'd slowly chipped away to find
a space for joy. Perhaps he tried to share
it with us too. Perhaps my grinding mind
just couldn't grow to grasp the gift he offered—
the life he's lifting up in laughter there.

The Return

Vancouver, on your skyline now the sun
descends and spreads—a blazing, bloody bath—
then drains. You stand unflinching through its wrath.
I watch and wonder, all down Highway 1:
that all my clean conclusions are undone,
that such life blossoms in the aftermath,
that I should—on this long and switchback path—
return again, though prodigal, a son.

Around me in the twilight now you pile
up a weight of presence I can't withstand.
The Hip on FM sing escape's at hand
for me, the travelling man. Let this last mile
stretch out to fill a year. Anchor my grand
illusions to your stubborn facts a while.

Hold to Mercy

Downstairs my kid is singing
of ants marching three by three.
His voice is dimly ringing
through suburban apathy—
so slight and thin and unrefined.
But will it sound so plain
when we're all driven underground,
escaping from the rain?
Who's built this grinding system
that these children will inherit?
Who's giving them the wisdom
and the inner strength to bear it?
He's singing eight by eight now
as toys rattle on the floor.
So hold to mercy,
lest you drive an angel from your door.

Now William Blake, it wasn't
just *these dark satanic mills*
that felt your voice of judgment.
You knew comfort slowly kills.
You heard loss in *the harlot's curse*—
it filled you full of rage
that you hammered out in fiery verse
across each painted page.
One day you blessed your angels
then you battled them the next—
like trying to untangle
hidden truths out of a text.
Well, any poet knows
to never trust a metaphor.
Just hold to mercy,
lest you drive an angel from your door.

I slummed here like a prophet
on a dirty greyhound bus
to tell the wealthy off, but
learned the wealthy are just us.
My anger's just the boredom
that the middle class has spun
around itself. It's more than
any greyhound can outrun.
We picked our fruit too early.
Now we're gnawing on the rinds.
If Blake were here he'd surely
etch some fire inside our minds.
He isn't, though. There's no one here
to help us anymore.
So hold to mercy,
lest you drive an angel from your door.

Rock on Rock on Voltaire Rousseau

Rock on rock on Voltaire Rousseau
'Cause revolution's all we know
We'll line them all up in a row
To build the kingdom here below

The line is long but we don't care
And when our turn comes in the square
We'll always meet it unaware
Rock on rock on Rousseau Voltaire

Rock on rock on Voltaire Rousseau
'Cause revolution's all we know
I guess we'll give it one more go
Rock on rock on Voltaire Rousseau

Against Granville Island

Come, all you migrant hippies, gather to these western shores.
I know a place to hide your wealthy birth.
Come, tormented yuppies, endless freedom can be yours.
You just need to remortgage your self-worth.

Renegades and tourists, come! And bring your aimless hopes.
In our harbour find a moment's rest.
Poets, drop your thick pretense and leap like antelopes!
On Granville Island no dreams are suppressed!

Granville, you have been to us a coffin and a crib,
a refuge from a world we can't endure.
Granville Bridge roars curving high above us like a rib,
but here the heart beats quiet and secure.

Granville, I have come to you, my poems and my coins
rattling in my pocket and my mind.
Vancouver! What anomaly is spawning from your loins?
How can you dare to keep it undefined?

Granville, you are wearing your self-image like a mask.
What is it you're so frightened to reveal?
Economy! I've seen your hand! You give us what we ask
while taking from us everything that's real.

Come, you wayward dreamers, rowed like vendors down the pier,
and open every spirit like a booth.
Yes, my friends, we live this lie in every moment here,
but in the hope it might become the truth.

Whatever Is Born in Fire

For my dad

1.

Saskatchewan toils quietly beneath a violent sweep of sky.
My parents have an acre south of Saskatoon
with more than its share of horizon.
And Dad and I, after the day's labour,
can sit out and watch the sky, in any direction,
descend in mysterious judgment on distant towns.
The lightning flashes across our vision
like a tear in the veil of time
while the heavy clouds gather to bring
the life-giving grain-loving rain.
The sun here, when it burns, burns hot and long.
In the morning, when it breaks the horizon, it does so
in a slow burst of flame.
And when it descends at day's end
it does so in much the same way—
a cataclysm of fire over the distant town of Conquest—
as if to say:
Whatever's born in fire will perish in fire.
The thought rolls to us slowly—
        where we sit out, drinking beer—
                like the thunder of another region.

2.

My Dad called me out to see one certain sunset
which rose red-rose into the skies,
which spread through the skyline, a slow-building onset
and blasted our day-wearied eyes.
But something else still, higher still than this dinning,
this fury the sun daily dies in:
two fate-borne jetstreams sank, spiralling, spinning,
down into the flaming horizon.
Who knew where they came from or where they were destined—
up where the thin ether can madden—
but in some bleak mindset they'd spun down and hastened
this flame-born flame-bound Armageddon.
The future was fiery and felt atmospheric,
an ending had finally begun,
and our minds were darkened with the Pink Floyd lyric:
Set controls for the heart of the sun.

3.
Come navigators, crewmen, gather closely, closely here
in the last cold lacerating light
of the failing flame-born engines.
Our dials are melting, our pilot is mad, our fuel is mostly fumes.
For us there is no final solace, no quiet descent into sleep.
Forged in the furnace of conquest and fear,
incubated in industry—

We can try to turn back—
      We could maybe turn back—
            And seek a strange new trajectory—

Or we must soar ahead—sear our hearts all to smoke.
Embark, and let our embers embrace
in the blinding, brimful, flame-blasted heart
of the fire-formed, fire-fated sun.

Clarence and Muriel

My grandma's name was Muriel.
My grandpa's name was Clarence.
Their families farmed Saskatchewan—
my parents' parents' parents.
Those generations worked the earth
where I'll join them in burial.
My grandpa's name was Clarence
and my grandma's name was Muriel.

When Muriel lived through the dustbowl
in the nineteen-thirties,
she learned that it takes heavy hustle
to breed the slimmest mercies.
Her father drifted off to search
for work out in the wind.
All she could do was wait and watch
his road to where it thinned.
That's how hope works—its secret currents
flow deep and mercurial.
That's how it was for Clarence.
That's how it was for Muriel.

And Clarence left his local schoolhouse
after the tenth grade.
The schoolbooks all felt flat and foolish.
Why would he have stayed?
Outside the window, wheat and oats
stood tall. He'd work to do.
And he still does. The harvest waits—
there's something wild and true
out in those pulsing fields of cereal,
past their swept appearance.
So go and find it, Muriel.
Go and find it, Clarence.

My grandma's name is Muriel.
My grandpa's name is Clarence.
Their families farmed Saskatchewan—
my parents' parents' parents.
Those generations worked the earth
where I'll join them in burial.
My grandpa's name is Clarence
and my grandma's name is Muriel.

Unblurring Vision

Maybe it's this simple. Maybe all we need is new eyes.

I looked over Vancouver this morning and I swear I glimpsed her angel, almost lost in the sunrise.

He hung over us all for the space of an intake of breath, with a wingspan as long as Hastings, as long as the aching horizon.

Then he thrust the air and rose swiftly, powerfully, to a distant point of light. And with his passage a gentle wind spread all through the breadth of Vancouver, smoothing its jagged edges, binding its sprawl together in the warmth of the morning.

I can't believe it took me so long to see the grace of the city. It guides us in such strange quiet ways. It channels our stubborn roads together until at last we recognize each other, and pause.

Maybe then, when we meet at last, I can explain to you what I've seen.

The Belltower Blues

A serious house on serious earth it is

—Philip Larkin

Back when I told you that I had a key
that could unlock that strange old creaky door
inside the vestment closet, where we'd find
a ladder and a hidden passageway
above the nave, and, where the passage ends,
the trapdoor to the belltower—we both knew
we'd grab some whiskey one night and go see.
That's how it is, sometimes, with such old friends.

The tower overlooks decaying rentals,
all being fast replaced by slim new-builds
in corrugated steel. That church still stands,
through all the frantic change outside its door:
so big, so needlessly ornate, and yet
unfinished—there's a gap where bells should be,
the metal redirected to the war.
I guess we're not immune to history.

We sat up there and laughed and swigged the bottle.
Night deepened, and we gradually became
part of the roofline, forged out of its frame.
The church stood tall, a grand anachronism,
bestowing on the minds of all who passed
its seriousness—though from that queasy height
I'd more incline to call it gravity.
No matter: We were there, and it seemed right.

Some morning, when developers come through
to clear that lot and build redundant condos,
they will not understand what they destroy.
That drafty holy space where many knew
their lives to focus in a vital moment.
That windy ledge, where we once sat like gargoyles—
our tear ducts streaming rain, our faces bent
so brightly in anachronistic joy.

The Writer's Retreat

Bless the Lord who has surrounded the traffic of human interest with the majesty of his law, who has given a direction to the falling leaf, and a goal to the green shoot.

—Leonard Cohen

Dedication

Old poet, I regret the years I've spent
beneath the heavy shadow of your verse.
Your lines are all—though strong and rich and terse—
a little dire, a little decadent.

We hurl our words up. They don't leave a dent—
deflecting off the heavens to disperse
like dust. These prayers just customise the curse:
I learned regret, but never to repent.

I always thought it was the law I broke
when I bent down to every word you spoke.
But look, the law still stands, unbroken, high
above this tangled valley where we choke
on dust and doubt and solitude and smoke.
I need to stand up too. At least I'll try.

The Hammer that Killed John Henry

John Henry was a man who saw
his hammer as his only law.
His back was straight, his arms were strong,
and as he worked he sang this song:

"A man ain't nothing but a man.
He'll do exactly what he can.
The little space where he is king
is circled by his hammer's swing."

That's the song he always sang,
him and his steel-driving gang,
shoulders swinging round like gears.
So he worked, for years and years.

Then one morning when he woke
he saw the sunrise full of smoke.
He turned to all the gathered folk
And wearily he sighed and spoke:

"Won't say it's pleasant, 'cause it's not,
but this hard work is all I've got.
You see that brand new factory?
That'll be the death of me.
           That'll be the death of me.
           That'll be the death of me."

Well, he worked harder, got more tired,
till the bossman said: "You're fired.
We've got a new steam engine can
work harder, faster than a man."

John Henry said: "That may well be,
but start it up and we will see.
I'll drop my hammer willingly
if that damn thing can outrace me."

They laid the rails and hammered hard.
The rails sang out, the hammers jarred.
John Henry swung like taking vengeance
on all damn steam-driven engines.

He finished just one length ahead,
his hammer handle dripping red.
He kissed it gently on the head
and with his dying breath he said:

"I worked with heart, I worked with ardour.
Machines work fast, they don't work harder.
Don't forget my dignity,
or that'll be the death of me.
> *That'll be the death of me.*
> *That'll be the death of me."*

This hammer killed John Henry, son.
But lay it down. Its day is done.
This relic from last century:
It won't kill me. It won't kill me.

"A man ain't nothing but a man"
just brings us back where we began.
But still it fills me up with dread
what Mississippi John Hurt said.

And Johnny Cash. And Woody Guthrie.
Those old singers, blues and country,
taught us how to die with pride.
And that's how all the heroes died.

Engines now control the land.
They took our work, and took command.
And dignity: that was the price
for this steam-driven paradise.

To sacrifice, you need a cause.
Integrity seeks deeper laws.
My helpless need to be more free:
That'll be the death of me.
> *That'll be the death of me.*
> *That'll be the death of me*

Freedom was Easy as Falling

No longer do I twist my back to watch
the gaping heavens flame and gleam and spark
I'm governed now by greyer smaller skies
that right my spine and lift my mind a notch

This city glinting in upon its port
each fine-cut edge of artifice and light
the strangeness of this landscape in the night
they murmur to me   of exile and rebirth

and of another time I knew before
this forge-steamed skyline and this iron shore
when the yoke of law seemed loosened from our backs
the earth gave up her fruit all out of season

and freedom was easy as falling   I escaped
I limped into the dusk to find a refuge
where my twisted frame could slowly be reshaped
I escaped   dragging my fractured backbone

The Life of the Lake

The lake likes what it likes. It leaves my legs
stepping out slowly through the cloying muck
and looks for some stonier surface to absorb.
It fingers up its mounded souvenirs
in shadowy quiet deep in its mildewy dredge.
Up past my knees the tide tugs at the edge
of all the life it holds here interlinked.
I skim my sight out where the surface shimmers
looking for subtle signs of other swimmers—
        the nameless anomalies
        piercing the landscape
        to stand up—damp dripping distinct.

I lie back in the lake and let it lift me.
The water laps and flicks against my ears
with dark and muffled murmuring. My eyesight
is straining in the daylight while mountainous clouds
spill upward through the spinning atmosphere—
immense—immeasurable. And down here
there's an unlaboured liberty in being small
as just a point of tension on a surface
that rings with wide and unfamiliar purpose—
        a piece of this peacefulness
        gifted and given
        alive in the life of it all.

The lake lives its own life. Alight with laughter
it whispers away the ridged and rigid world
in limitless and everlasting liquid
while I drift unlooking back toward the land.
The far shore is a faded blue-grey—formless
in the fluid distance. My feet feel around for firmness—
for the certainty of my own solid state.
And I hope I don't forget this—to be grateful
when I feel the ground grow firm before my footfall—
        when the fitful mercurial
        movements of matter
        are gathered to welcome my weight.

The Landscaper

He stands in a park in the suburbs,
bewildered. His shoulders are squared grimly,
his brows knotted, his mouth locked in a scowl
that quivers against despair. His clothes
are streaked with grass mulchings and dog filth.
Billowing smoke in front of him, like an altar,
an ancient tractor mower has come
to a final and long-deserved rest.

He couldn't even tell you how it ended
if you asked. He's strong and stubborn
and works like a mule. Yet the grass
that blankets the hills and medians
of his city always came out looking
coarse and uneven. Whatever he tried,
his kind thick hands seemed to push too hard
on the wrong button. He always thought
he'd find a job where his strength of arm
and of will would bring some kind of value.
Perhaps. He hasn't found it yet.

The lawn tractor is strong, and it has taken
him all summer to kill, but now at last
it has ground to its uttermost halt.
Blue smoke bulges out and spreads into the wind.

His eyes are still held by the smoldering hulk
that stands as a monument to the inevitable failure
of all he attempts in this world, but they won't be
held for much longer. Soon he'll wrench them away,
and he'll turn his back on that smoking wreckage
as firmly and as finally as he's turned his back
so many times before. He's smart enough
to know that, not so long ago, strength
and simplicity and singleness of mind were valued.
And he's wise enough to know those days are past.
He'll walk away toward the bus stop,
and he won't look back. The sun will be setting

gloriously behind him, igniting the tractor's
dull blue smoke in rich and ancient colours.
And in the gathering darkness above him
shooting stars will crisscross in the sky—
and you'll swear that they're all dying satellites,
circuits fused, flaming down through the atmosphere,
gears grinding into silence,
overwhelmed by the clarity of this man's soul.

The Writer's Retreat

Tonight I bar the door and square my seat.
My one friend's gone to Calgary or Guelph
or some damn place, and left me to myself,
in solitude and scholarly retreat.
Tonight I write! My catalogue complete:
typewriter, great books spilling from the shelf,
old dishes, clothes, the heart's appalling pelf,
the genius, the pride, the self-deceit.

Now silence swells. The mind shines like a jewel,
the page with all the promise of a dream.
What self-control! What will! My fearless rule!
For life is my most elementary school.
A noise out in the hall: "Shut up!" I scream,
and catapult a string of angry drool.

Broken Invocation

Muse, I have seen you in the distant east of evening skies, sliding down the wave-crest of night.

The light was poor and my eyes—wearied and bloodshot from my long vigil—had known better hours. But I stood dramatically backlit by the sunset and certainly I saw you. Did you happen to see me? I like to think that the light was accentuating my profile.

To whom were you carried by the advancing black surf? You rode with such grace, the first stars flying about you like flecks of foam, and when you cut across the face of the wave you were slicing east from west and night from day. Then you slipped away from sight and, however briefly, I actually thought you were coming to me.

But I should have known better. Yours is an arbitrary administration. You choose whomever you choose, and then rarely for very long.

I know I have called upon you before with arrogance and impatience. But all that is drained out of me tonight. Now nothing remains but my desperation and my aching need.

Please hear me. I will lay out for you dripping sacrifices of flesh. I will leave you milk and cookies. I will scatter first editions around my tiger trap. Please save me from obscurity and triviality. Please give me something I can sell to pay my internet bill.

You know where to find me, like you've always known.

But you never have.

Homer's the only one you've truly loved.

The Satellites that Serve Us

Hey pretty, let's leave the city tonight.
Let's see if there's something to see.
It can't be as dull as the suburbs. Not quite.
It can't be as flat as TV.

We'll drive till your phone loses all of its bars.
We'll drive till the orderly headlights of cars
fade out, and there's nothing but high ancient stars.

But artifice hides even up in the heights:
The satellites …

The satellites that serve us
swing their gravity out wide
and tug on us to swerve us back inside.

Hey darling, you never stop startling me.
Here we stand on this starlit terrain
and you still want to think that the city is free.
Have they planted a chip in your brain?

Take a look at this landscape that lifts its lament
while the eyes of society, cold, diligent,
lean closer in gradual blazing descent,

drawn downward, still fixing our souls in their sights:
The satellites!

The satellites that serve us
will come crashing from the void
while we wait here, wired, nervous, paranoid.

Hey baby, you tell me, and maybe you're right,
that we've work to do while we're still here—
that silence encompasses us, and the night
waits like some huge unknowable ear.

But all of our work's just resulted in this:
the careless invention, the wild avarice
that flings out our signal into the abyss.

You say that's all purged when one pure thought ignites
the satellites …

The satellites that serve us
burn our dreams across the skies.
But our dreams will not deserve us till they rise.

Nepotism Also Slams It Open

This may not be the entrance you were hoping—
nose pressed against the door closed in your face.
But
        nepotism also slams it open.
Sometimes these things can operate both ways.

Mundane Monday

Another mundane Monday brings
stale coffee and an early meeting.
There's mercy in the midst of things—
it's often absent, but it sends
an out-of-office email that
is full of words that look important.
I'm somehow still left feeling flat
        when mundane Monday ends.

The printer's jammed, and tech support
has never really been supportive.
I work by hand to stack and sort
the briefings, while my mind ascends
to all I'd like to make and share,
and how I'll fill with work and value
the bleary hour I'll have to spare
        when mundane Monday ends.

We crowd to get aboard the bus
at 5 PM, or sometimes later.
They'd never hold a space for us:
No, not for anyone who spends
their rationed days on this bright earth
adhering to a filing system.
We'll all know what our time was worth
        when mundane Monday ends.

The days seem like a cycle, but
more often they just build momentum
that spills toward I-don't-know-what—
I guess as always it depends
on how we meet the slow despair
that greets us by the water cooler.
These choices will be with us there
        when mundane Monday ends.

They say they'll know us by our fruits
but sometimes growth won't see the surface.
When pruned back did we put down roots?
Or is this bitterness that bends
in on itself how we'll receive
the grace of being ordinary?
The shape we hold here's how we'll leave
        when mundane Monday ends.

Imminence

Though he is the same in his substance,
In his law, toward us, he changes.

—St. Ephrem the Syrian

The Lonesome Blues

We'll say the lonesome blues drove us to drive
this distance—Ottawa to Winnipeg.
We'll say they weighed the heart that weighed the leg
that weighed the gas, through hour twenty-five.
We'll say we got here, worn-down, but alive,
then couldn't stay. We'll keep our reasons vague:
We don't commit for fear we might renege.
We'll say we just weren't ready to arrive.

And silence will then settle like a bruise
upon our past. But now, as dusk descends
in seeping indigo, it frees two friends
from loss, from love, from all we fear to lose.
We flicker, as the highway shifts and bends,
then turn and blur into the lonesome blues.

The Vengeance of the Tennessee Waltz

I was dancing with my darling to the Tennessee Waltz.
Her eyes were shining like new coins, lost in the vaults.
But I'm high in expenditures and short on results
while I'm dancing with my darling to the Tennessee Waltz.

Our minds are in the sky and we're knee-deep in schmaltz
and we're filled up with those secrets that you hide from adults,
until the music groans slower as the turntable halts
and leaves us grasping at the chasm of the Tennessee Waltz.

Here the warm heart collapses, here the dark mind exults,
as we stagger out a three-step over tectonic faults.
But it'll grind us to fine dust and mineral salts,
the primordial triplets of the Tennessee Waltz.

It's the mystery of mysteries, the occult of occults,
that drags the spirit down toward the heart's inner vaults,
but then something short-circuits and the backlash assaults
our senses with the vengeance of the Tennessee Waltz.

I was dancing with my darling to the Tennessee Waltz,
and the melody it moved through us just like a pulse.
But our gestures, our messages all proved to be false—
these ill-at-ease formalities—this Tennessee Waltz.

Beneath the bright and blunted night, beneath our dark malts,
we lacked the skill, the strength of will, to act like adults.
She turned and walked away. Reset the defaults:
Self-pity, malt whiskey, and the Tennessee Waltz.

Song for Solitary Voice

I now write songs for solitary voice.
I've given up the world, gripped with disgrace.
Appalled how hunger hollows out a face,
I turned alone and made my solemn choice.
I came to you and found again this clois-
tering of wills, this vaulted empty space.
I'm hauled through the abyss of your great grace,
then left here, stricken, straining to rejoice.

But tell me now please if this world apart
can hold a home, a family, a wife,
to stir my space and shift my sodden heart;
or, in this clarity, as dreams depart,
allow this lonely, long, productive life
to gather its slow bulk, and make a start.

Hymn # 735

We quietly prayed for a miracle
while we suffered and laboured and sinned.
At moments our prayers became lyrical.
At times they screamed into the wind.
God remained holy and distant
while history turmoiled and tossed.
It could be that we were resistant.
It could be that we were just lost.

We quietly prayed for a miracle
while the bulldozers broke through the wall.
When the value of life is empirical
can it have any value at all?
We cried out in desperate chorus.
Our voices felt loud and obscene,
while voices of all those before us
rang distantly through the machine.

We quietly prayed for a miracle
whatever the centuries said.
When they told us the world was spherical.
When they told us that Jesus was dead.
A voice offered vague consolation
then faded out into the gloom.
So we stand after each generation,
expectant ears pressed to a tomb.

Deflation

In this room, the wreckage of my days
is tossed about and spilling from the hamper.
Outside the sun is brooding like a vampire
        behind the winter haze.

I must have sprung a leak. I once was full
of life. Now I'm deflating. Here's the problem:
it won't be long before my spinal column
        cannot support my skull.

The weight that's in my head will have me pinned
down in this heap I'm fast collapsing into.
Now, too late, I'm wishing that my window
        was open to the wind.

Someone say a name I could invoke
to send a breath and lift me from this torment,
flapping, flailing, like an empty garment
        lost in the distant smoke.

The Day in Slow Ascent

I can marvel now
at the sheer complexity of design
that these few waking hours should harbour
so many systematically shattered
dreams of success.
And the hurt has not diminished but
it is accompanied by
a quiet battered gratitude
to have been once again brought so forcefully
back into focus
by the hammer of perspective.

Still I can't seem to help remarking
a little bitterly
what a fitting end to the day it is
when this city bus grumbles and groans on westward
past the northbound road I had thought
was supposed to carry me to Vespers
and my one remaining consolation.

And with a sigh I lean back upon
your hidden providence
and the long mysterious arc of transit.

In the sky ahead
the declining sun flashes behind a tangle of clouds
and my heart
wearied by the daylight's struggles
can hardly bear this final glory.

And I wish this pale and final light could be gathered up
into a sponge sopping red and gold
to wipe clear for once
the opacity of the world we move through.

And I know that in just a blink
it would be smeared again.

But grant us these few seconds to glimpse
our ever-forgotten destination
and perhaps to mark this day
with its sorrows and its troubles and its echoing failure
in a slow and microscopic ascent
as the bus lurches late at a light
and swings widely toward the north.

The Junkman of Regrets

The daybreak here is smothered, thin and cold.
It bleeds a clouded light on mute withdrawn
horizons, but no warmth, no colour. Dawn
just fizzles out, without a glint of gold.

All day these hopes collide. Steel frames enfold
each other, grasping, gasping, till they're gone.
And evening spreads its thoughtless light upon
their tangled wrecks—more than a heart can hold.

And that's when I begin. I haul and shove
these jagged shards—aluminum, steel, tin—
into a rusted heap that groans above
the clouded dawn. I work—the junkman of
regrets—for their rebirth, some morning, in
this incremental alchemy of love.

Blessing

You whimper and stir, deep in the darkness,
dreams sprawling wide through your unmapped mind.
I reach out to touch you, just lightly, the presence
of someone else as you face into the wind.

Then your hands are on mine. Your small fragile fingers
are gripping my hand, strangely strongly. Secure
just to sense me, you sigh. I breathe out this blessing
to you—then and now—who you are, who you were:

You're safe here and warm as
your first muffled darkness—
so small and so carefully curled.
gently unclench all
your unfelt potential
and softly wake into the world.

The Life We Chose

It's nice to share a bed again,
even if it's just like this—
jammed on this twin mattress, in
a room our toddler's claimed as his.
He lies in a triumphant sprawl,
with starred-out arms and legs and head.
He somehow spreads to smother all
the surface of our double bed.
But we're just happy he's asleep,
and maybe soon we might be too.
And, crammed right up against your hip,
I'm thankful to be next to you.

Our other kid's in his own room
asleep, but soon, like every night,
he'll wake and call for me to come.
There's not much I can do but wait.
And when he calls of course I'll go,
and once I'm there I'll probably stay—
collapsed, exhausted—though I'll know
you're right here—just a room away.
So even though I doubt I'll sleep
wedged on this mattress on the floor,
this moment's one I want to keep.
I'll lie here just a little more.

We've made our choices. What we chose
is this. We'll see what this can be
with time and love. Tomorrow is
our ten-year anniversary.
Life moves so fast, but it's immense.
It's rolled out like a long cascade
of choices, sometimes packed so dense
we're not quite certain which we've made.
But here it's brought us—to our sons,
and to this hollow, dragging night.
Some choices you don't make just once—
you choose and then you hold on tight.

Is there another life we could
have chosen? I don't think I care.
How would it do us any good
to have a life unlived out there?
Each choice is like an offramp burned,
or like a seed that falls and dies.
Some were intended, others weren't,
but I won't wish them otherwise.
When dawn creeps round our blackout blinds,
I'll face it thankful you're my wife.
Whatever flaws the fresh day finds,
I'll choose and choose and choose this life.

A kid's voice whimpers from the dark.
You stir—you'd just begun to doze.
The voice fades out and you sink back
to sleep. This is the life we chose.
And though there's always more to do,
as we rush round from task to task,
we're raising up an answer to
the questions there's no time to ask—
like what our life's created of,
and what our life's created for.
These choices build to form our love.
I'll lie here just a little more.

Too Much Morningtime

Inexplicably awake,
your small voice seems to fill the night,
narrating the undreamt darkness.
Buoyant boy, your brain is bright—
brimming words and bursting wide,
a poet at the age of three.
I can't forget that time you said
There's too much morningtime in me,
explaining why you once again
were waking in a world that slept.
This sudden need for passing on
the words that rattle in your depth—
it's new to you. You don't know yet
how silence slowly floods a man.
Insomniac child, wide-eyed wordsmith,
speak now while you can.

The 613

A winter night in Ottawa is monstrous.
The wind shrieks down between these empty towers
abandoned by the bureaucrats now safe
and warm at home. My fingers, cold and stiff,
are fumbling for my phone. In these bleak hours,
I've made some desperate calls. Here, no one answers.

We're lost beneath this restless regulation.

Near Parliament, at Wellington and Bank,
I tap out six-one-three, our area code,
then pause, uncertain, till my phone goes blank.

—

Some old Rabbinic scholars, analyzing
the Torah, counted out its laws. The number
by most accounts: six hundred and thirteen.
To me, the whole attempt feels small and thin—
so focused on the gold that plates the altar,
you fail to see the fiery pillar rising.

It's not so simple, though. The Psalmist knew:

The law has life. It's more than normative.
It is a gateway, opening to offer
a wide abundant space in which to live.

—

The snow plows pile the stubborn winter rubble
up off the road. The city's raw and worn.
I tried to leave, but lost my only chance.
So here I stay, in vague obedience.
But spring is seeping. Water drips. I turn
to feel warm light through mounds of ice and gravel.

They slowly soften, in the sun's repentance.

And I will grow to thank the living law
which forced my will, and held me here to glimpse
this inward-spreading spring: the heart's slow thaw.

Acknowledgements

The title "The Living Law" was suggested to me many years ago by the late and much loved Canadian poet Steven Heighton. We were discussing a stack of sonnets I'd given him to review, when he was Writer in Residence at the University of Ottawa, and he pointed to that phrase in particular as one I should develop. Over the subsequent decade, that discussion gradually began to give shape to this book. I have found the idea of a "living law" to be a useful shorthand for the thematic content gathered here, which often deals with the vibrant boundaries of human experience. Just as importantly, I have found it a helpful metaphor for thinking about the generative constraints of poetic form. I always thought I would write to Steven and thank him for his advice. I waited too long, and he died in 2022. I hope this book can stand as one small memorial to his thoughtful generosity.

Many of the poems included here have been published elsewhere, sometimes in slightly different forms. "Beneath the Buzzing of my Brainstem," "A Strand of Sound," and "A Hermit's Elegy" first appeared in *Ekstasis Magazine*. "The Boatwright" first appeared in *Blue Unicorn*. "Sunrise Over Crow Puddle" and "The Life We Chose" first appeared in *THINK: A Journal of Poetry, Fiction, and Essays*. "Lightning Strikes Churches" was a third-place winner of the Kierkegaard Poetry Competition and was published in both the magazine *Dappled Things* and the anthology *Homage to Søren Kierkegaard: Poems in Memory of Reverend Ronald Marshall* from Wiseblood Books. "Villanelle of the Elect" was reprinted in *Solum Journal*, after initial publication by *Darkly Bright Press*. "The Life of the Lake" was first published in *Cloud Lake Literary*. "Nepotism Also Slams It Open" was first published on *Asses of Parnassus*. "The Lonesome Blues" was first published in *The Orchards Poetry Journal*. "Too Much Morningtime" was first published in *Better than Starbucks*. In addition, the following poems were first published online by *Darkly Bright Press*: "The Living Law," "Mid-Lent," "The Eleventh Hour," "After Psalm 73," "Hospitality," "Praise Him with Clashing Symbols," "The Belltower Blues," "Mundane Monday," and "The 613".

The epigram from St. Ephrem the Syrian is taken from Jeffrey T. Wickes' translation of *The Hymns on Faith*. Biblical references are mostly to the *Revised Standard Version*, though there is also a strong influence from Donald Sheehan's translation of *The Psalms of David*. The italicized lines in "Highway 17 Revisited" are direct quotations from Bob Dylan's album *Highway 61 Revisited*. The italicized lines in "Hold to Mercy," and the title of "Rock on Rock on Voltaire Rousseau," are references to various William Blake poems. Much of the language in "The Hammer that Killed John Henry," including the title, is inspired by Mississippi John Hurt's song "Spike Driver Blues" and Woody Guthrie's version of "John Henry." The title "The Satellites that Serve Us" is taken from a 1983 issue of *National Geographic* I found in a box, and the image of a giant ear is borrowed from Emily Dickinson's "I Felt a Funeral, in my Brain." While "Mid-Lent" is not a strict Golden Shovel, it is certainly indebted to Terrance Hayes' innovation in the form.

This book is a compilation of poems written over 20 years, and more people have had a hand in the work than I can possibly list here. I'm grateful to the *Darkly Bright Press* community for their support and constructive feedback on these poems, particularly Christopher Tompkins, Joshua Alan Sturgill, and Fr. Anthony Gilbert. Many of the older poems were first developed through collaborations with artists in music, film, and theatre—namely Landon A. R. Coleman, Jeremy Eisenhauer, Aaron Zenga, and Steven Bourque. My old friend Mark Josefson inspired several of these poems, and I dedicate to him every poem with "blues" in the title.

Finally, my love and thanks to my family for their ongoing support. Thanks to my parents, who have always supported my writing. Thanks to my sons for inspiring many of these poems and leaving me little pockets of time to write and edit. And above all thanks to my wife, Kat, whose love and encouragement makes all of this possible.

About the Poet

Jesse Keith Butler lives with his wife and two children in Ottawa, Ontario. He recently completed a PhD in Education, which led to his current work in the Canadian civil service. His poetry has been published in various Canadian and American journals, and he recently was a third place winner in the Kierkegaard Poetry Competition. This is his first book.

www.ingramcontent.com/pod-product-compliance
Lightning Source LLC
Chambersburg PA
CBHW051638120626
46551CB00014B/2122